The Other Side of the Fire

The Other Side of the Fire

SECOND EDITION

JAN R. ADAMS M.D.

The Other Side of the Fire
Copyright © 2020 by Jan R. Adams M.D. All rights reserved.

No part of this publication may be reproduced, stored in a retrieval system or transmitted in any way by any means, electronic, mechanical, photocopy, recording or otherwise without the prior permission of the author except as provided by USA copyright law.

The opinions expressed by the author are not necessarily those of URLink Print and Media.

1603 Capitol Ave., Suite 310 Cheyenne, Wyoming USA 82001
1-888-980-6523 | admin@urlinkpublishing.com

URLink Print and Media is committed to excellence in the publishing industry.

Book design copyright © 2020 by URLink Print and Media. All rights reserved.

Published in the United States of America

Library of Congress Control Number: 2020917365
ISBN 978-1-64753-475-2 (Paperback)
ISBN 978-1-64753-476-9 (Digital)

30.07.20

For DRC
"You fill up my senses"
JD

"When love beckons to you, follow him,
Though his ways are hard and steep...

...But If In your fear you would seek only
love's peace and love's pleasure,
Then it is better for you that you cover
your nakedness and pass out of love's
threshing-floor,
Into the seasonless world where you
shall laugh, but not all of your laughter,
and weep, but not all of your tears.

Kahlil Gibran
The Prophet

GOD IS BEING, not "A BEING". As SHE Is all there Is. As HE Is everything.

GOD'S LOVE is eternal, dependable, unconditional, and complete. Let me repeat that: GOD'S LOVE is eternal, dependable, unconditional, and complete.

That TRUTH can be very difficult to remember since we have been taught the contrary since birth. We have been trained to believe the opposite. We have been conditioned to believe that GOD'S LOVE Is doled out as a teacher would assign grades, or a parent would offer praise. It Is not. GOD'S LOVE IS eternal, dependable, unconditional, and complete.

That is a tremendous revelation coming from me. Do not take it lightly. I arrived here after a lifetime of mistakes, bad judgments, and frankly shameful, behaviors. I am embarrassed that my Journey has taken so long. But, I am convinced that GOD grants us all forgiveness so that we might live a grander vision of ourselves. One in which our actions are motivated by our higher self: "a life motivated by love and guided by knowledge".

At a time in my life when I expected to enjoy the fruits of my labors, life collapsed. I found myself in a hole that I could not have imagined in my most horrible of nightmares. I was lost. My soul was bankrupt.

I considered all manner of solutions. Most of them were centered in selfishness and anger. There are the seeds of good and evil in all of us.

GOD'S LOVE, during the worst time of my life, provided me with the guidance and direction I so desperately needed. There is peace, and love, on the other side of tragedy.

I am grateful for HER LOVE. I am thankful for HIS GRACE. There is no tragedy that GOD'S LOVE cannot, and will not, conquer.

Introduction

From our personal and myopic point of view, we live in troubled times. Terrorism, financial collapse, religious wars, famine and pandemics are the norm. Fear not, for there have always been challenges to man's survival here on Earth and the answer lies where it has always lain: in faith.

Phillip's story is a simple tale. In it is a portion of every man's (and every nations) story and so its message is powerful. Many of the images he presents may be painful or even difficult for you to accept. You may recognize in his failures some of your own. You may come to realize that behaviors you once thought innocent were in fact, the cause for much of your own unhappiness.

Fear not! For Phillip's story will also remind you of the power of GOD'S LOVE. You will leave it with the tools necessary for turning a tragedy into triumph. You will leave it with the courage to continue your journey through life with confidence for success.

You are your own rule maker. You set the guidelines. The true intentions of your SOUL are known only to you. For you, and only you, can decide who and what you really are, and who and what you really want to be.

You are in control. Resist the notion that there is someone, or something, doing it to you. You are the captain of your ship. You are in charge.

Therefore, only you can decide how well you are doing. No one else can judge you.

Life is a process of creation. There is nothing to learn for life is not a process of discovery. Consciousness and remembering are the only tools you will need.

We are one, you and I. We are not separate from each other, nor are we separate from GOD.

Phillip, a man who believed he was separate from everything, came to accept that his life was defined by tragedy. It was, and is, not.

As you read, hear the wisdom in his story. Take from Phillip that which serves you. Know that his story is your story; an inspiration for us all.

Life is all of it, the good and the bad. It is the pleasure and the pain. It is the Joy and the sadness. It is the ups and the downs.

"Therefore, be a light unto the darkness, and curse it not. Forget not who you are in the moment of your encirclement by that which you are not. Inquire within, rather than without. For the experience you create is the statement of who you are and who you choose to be. Know that what you do in the time of your greatest trial, can be the creation of your greatest triumph."

YHWH

> GOD SPEAKS TO ALL OF US, ALL THE TIME.
> THE REAL QUESTION IS NOT TO WHOM DOES GOD SPEAK, BUT WHO LISTENS.

If you believe as Phillip had come to believe: that 'HELL' does not exist as a place, but rather as a condition. One in which the results of your actions do not exist in harmony with your greatest expectations. Then surely 'HELL' is where he was.

Phillip doubted not only his own thoughts about his worth as a person, but also his connection to GOD and any plan HE might have for him.

Phillip's life had fallen apart. His career was in shambles. He had completely isolated himself from friends and colleagues. And, to top it off, the woman he loved had abandoned him. Phillip never saw it coming and so, understandably, he was devastated.

Phillip had convinced himself that he had done everything correctly. He had prepared and trained well for his job. He had followed through on every opportunity. His motives were honorable. His efforts were actually designed to have something to give back to his family and to the world community. Just when it seemed he would reap the benefits of his labors, it all fell apart.

It was not surprising then that, from time to time, Phillip even resented GOD for being alive. He had lived his entire life with heart disease. He took four to five different medications a day. That alone should have resulted in his death by the time he was forty. Yet he had pressed on, paying particular attention to his diet, exercise, and rest. He had persevered.

Two years earlier, Phillip had developed pulmonary emboli that surely should have killed him. He spent four weeks in a coma that time. His saving grace: his obsession with cardiovascular conditioning. Without the extra lung reserves there would not have been enough oxygen to keep him alive. The result was something that he could deal with: just one more medicine, a blood thinner.

There were times when reason compelled Phillip to admit that it was stupid for him to resent GOD. He often joked that GOD was more of a failure than he was. For he, Phillip, was still standing. GOD had missed two opportunities to take his life.

Yet, GOD, a failure, was more than even Phillip was prepared to swallow… even in his most cynical of times. What purpose could there possibly be in that? What was God's plan here? The universe, it would seem, was not unfolding exactly as it should.

His misery reached its zenith shortly thereafter. Phillip was invited to lunch by a segment producer for CBS's 'Good Morning America'. His attorney and he met her at Spago, Wolfgang Puck's restaurant in Beverly Hills. The purpose was to discuss Phillip's appearance on their show.

The atmosphere was surreal. Phillip was physically present and yet, seemed to watch their meeting as a spectator from two tables removed. She, this producer, seemed genuinely concerned that (he) "had to feel devastated".

After all, (he) had been "on top of the world" (as she had put it) "a plastic surgeon in Beverly Hills with a TV show, a skincare line, and books on plastic surgery. Yet in an instant, the press (according to her) "had taken it all away. Surely", she kept repeating (over and over again), "you have to be devastated and people want to hear your side."

Phillip wasn't devastated though, he was worst. He was numb, and sadly, didn't have a side, not even his own. She was also wrong about what people wanted. People didn't want to hear his side. They ignored the facts. People were looking for an opportunity to confirm their basest beliefs. No amount of truth was going to interfere with that. Philip declined to do their show.

A few days later a reporter with WDTN in Dayton, Ohio, contacted Phillip through a close friend. She was producing a story with a local twist and was concerned that "some of the elements of the story just didn't seem to fit". She was looking to see if he could "fill in the holes" for her.

Phillip and the reporter exchanged niceties and the interview progressed as most interviews do. Then suddenly, the interviewer interrupted the flow of the conversation. "You seem so calm and confident" she said. "If I were in your shoes, I'd be a mess. What's your secret? I'm a single mom with two boys, and I'd like to pass on to them something to help them deal with adversity".

She was wise indeed.

Phillip paused for a moment. There was no secret. At least, to be honest, he hadn't really thought about it. He did, however, have a moment of Divine clarity: "GOD", he thought, "SPEAKS TO ALL OF US, ALL THE TIME. THE REAL QUESTION IS NOT TO WHOM DOES GOD SPEAK, BUT WHO LISTENS."

"I do not doubt GOD'S intentions", Phillip said to her. "I believe that GOD can be trusted. I believe that GOD'S love can be depended on, and I believe that GOD'S acceptance is unconditional. The outcome is NOT in question.

I listen to the voice within me "he said".

"You can view a tragedy, such as this, as a curse, or a gift. And how you perceive it, is what it will be. There are no villains, nor victims, in GOD'S world.

One can choose to be that 'angry' person who is the result of what has happened, or one can choose to be the person they are as a result of doing, and being, something about what has happened. I chose the latter."

That was the extent of his advice to her, and the silence at the other end of the phone proved that was all that was needed.

> "All SAINTS HAVE A PAST, AND All SINNERS HAVE A FUTURE!"

Phillip had not always lived with that level of consciousness. As I remember it, when we met, he was spiritually bankrupt. He was overwhelmed with self-pity and self-doubt. Which I might add, is never good. Self-pity leads to self-hate, and self-hate leads to self-destructive behavior. Phillip was ... well... let me start at the beginning:

When Phillip regained consciousness, he was understandably confused. "Where am I?" he thought. "How did I get here? All he could remember was falling, no jumping, from his office window.

Phillip had reached a point in his life of where he could no longer live with himself. As he plummeted toward the ground, his entire life rocketed through his consciousness. When he arrived in my presence, he was exhausted and completely lost as to where he was. "Where am I?" he thought. How did I get here? Am I dead? Is this heaven?"

Phillip clearly had more questions than answers. However, he did not hurt as no bones were broken, was not cold, thirsty, or hungry and so drifted back into his exhaustion, back to what could only be described as sleep.

His "second awakening" however, was not so peaceful. A flash of blinding light yanked him into consciousness. The shear pain of it all engulfed his entire body. Every cell screamed with the shock of being blasted into the present. It was as if he had fallen into the center of a volcano and in a flash been burned to a crisp.

He was disoriented and afraid. That is why Phillip watched silently as a little old man dressed in a white lab coat went feverishly about his work. Phillip dared not interrupt, and so was content to only observe.

The old man's posture exposed his many years. His torso was flexed 90 degrees at the waist. This accentuated the curve in his spine suggesting that he might possibly be carrying the weight of the world on his shoulders.

Phillip continued to stare at him in disbelief. He rubbed his eyes again and made an effort to look at things more clearly. "Somehow", he thought, "my mind must be playing tricks on me."

What an odd picture this old man presented. He was nothing less than a bag of contradictions. The black three-piece suit that he wore under his white starched lab coat was disheveled, as was his soft blue shirt. Yet his black silk tie was immaculate. Even his shoes contrasted the remainder of his costume. They too were impeccable just like his tie.

His posture and disheveled manner of dress, however, proved to be in direct odds with his spirit. "Hello," he said almost singing. "You really gave me a scare there for a moment."

Phillip strained again to wake himself. He had struggled before trapped in dreams where his mind was awake, but he was unable to move his body. He had to snap out of this "trick" that his mind was playing on him. He jerked himself up and focused once more on the little old man. There was no doubt about it. This was not Phillip's imagination. This man was real.

"Where am I? Who are you?" Phillip asked. "How did I get here?"

"You got here step by step. You chose to be here" the old man answered. "Not consciously mind you, but nonetheless, it was your decision."

"My decision ?" Phillip asked.

"Yes...yours!"

Phillip paused for a moment, once more taking in his surroundings. "Where is here?" he thought. 'Where exactly, am I?" The old man smiled warmly at Phillip, "You're exactly half-way home."

"Half-way home?" How would he know that?" Phillip thought. "I've never seen him or this place before. He couldn't possibly know where home is. How could he know anything about me?"

"I know more than you think," the old man interrupted. "But we'll get to that. Your journey has been a long one with many twists and turns. You must be hungry. How about I get you something to eat? We'll talk over dinner".

In an adjacent room a magnificent table was set with all of Phillip's favorites. There was grilled salmon, sautéed spinach and mashed potatoes. A beet salad sat to the side and a chocolate cake was in the middle of the table. "This is too weird. How could he know all this? Where did this food come from?"

As they sat at the table the old man offered Phillip water and continued with his explanation, "Like I said, you're half way home. I'm here to help with the rest of your journey. I realize that you have spent a lifetime dabbling in spiritual growth, but the truth is you have not really been committed to it."

Phillip considered the old man's words carefully ... "I must be dead," he thought.

The old man continued without missing a beat, "It was about a year ago, give or take a few months, when you realized that, in spite of all the outward suggestions of success, you were miserable. Not miserable like you were having a bad day because your Rolls Royce needed repair, or a flight to Monaco had been delayed. I'm talking about miserable to the point of wanting out, of wanting to die.

I'm talking about miserable to the point of waking in the morning at 5:00 am and laying there in the fetal position until noon. I am talking about rising not because you could think of something to do, but rather because you could no longer take being alone with your own thoughts.

Starting every day with dread like that is horrifying. Waking to a feeling of emptiness, exhausted by eight hours of sleep is more than anyone should have to bear."

Phillip could not hide his concern. "No doubt about it, I'm dead. This must be…GOD?"

"The scary part, "the old man continued, "is that at some level you had convinced yourself that it was all normal. Yet what is normal about hopelessness?

You did not speak about it, your misery, not even to your friends. To do so would have destroyed the illusion of happiness you had so carefully constructed around yourself. To do so would have destroyed the illusion of perfection that was so needed to survive in the world in which you had chosen to live. But why choose to live a lie?"

Phillip stared at the old man in disbelief…and awe. "Who is he and how is he privy to my most private thoughts?"

"They are not that private, believe me" the old man added. "You may choose to believe so, but to anyone willing to really look, it's quite obvious. The sadness that surrounds your every step is unmistakable. A child could see the sorrow in your eyes that you hide behind a smile."

Phillip nodded in quiet agreement. "You're probably right", he confessed, "but honestly I can't even begin to tell you how I got this way. I'm not even sure myself how I got here."

"You got here surely and steadily" offered the old man. "The truth is that your path was more direct than most. Your ticket was your misery. You have referred to it by different names: anger, depression, resentment, hate, guilt, or jealousy. You have associated it with different events from time to time also. But its origin lies in one condition: THE EMPTINESS AND DESPAIR THAT IS ASSOCIATED WITH THE FEELING OF INCOMPLETENESS

THAT ACCOMPANIES THE LOSS OF AWARENESS OF ONES CONNECTION TO GOD."

"Wow" thought Phillip, "That was a mouthful. "He then turned directly to face the old man, "What on earth are you talking about?"

"I'm talking about you" said the old man shaking his head as he continued. "The really sad part is that you, and others like you, believe you are alone. You believe that this state of affairs is happening only to you.

You have come to think of it as normal because so many of you have engaged in this thinking. Under those conditions it may be seen as normal, but I can assure you that it is not natural. It was never intended that human beings should think this way of themselves."

In the last few years Phillip had come to spend a lot more time questioning his life. The feeling that he was in no way living the life he had intended to live was a constant distraction. But he had never contributed his failures, or his unhappiness, to a lack of awareness of his connection to GOD. "No one ever does" said the old man.

Phillip Ignored that.

However, he had spent his time looking for reasons for his unhappiness outside of himself. There was always something, or someone else whose behavior had been less than exemplary. An ex-girlfriend, an uncle, or some authority figure had all served themselves up as convenient scapegoats. "Why not blame God", Phillip had thought. "Maybe this old man has something here". Phillip hadn't been very happy, or very successful, in blaming other people. GOD, it would seem, had been the greatest disappointment of them all. "Why shouldn't he finally step forward and be counted as the perpetrator of Phillip's misery?

"Well you could", offered the old man.

"Could what?" asked Phillip.

"Blame GOD. Unfortunately though, that would not solve your dilemma. We both know that the solution lies somewhere inside of you. GOD has given you the tools. Your job is to use them."

Phillip sat suspended in disbelief "Where am I?" he wondered again. "And how is this old man always in my head?"

> YOU ARE NOT YOUR MIND,
> NOR ARE YOU YOUR THOUGHTS,
> YOU ARE NOT EVEN YOUR BODY;
> YOU ARE YOUR SOUL!

"It is not me, but you, who are always in your head," offered the old man. "That is precisely the problem. You are in your head."

"What does that mean?" asked Phillip.

"You know exactly what it means. You initially recognized your unhappiness and misery as a teenager. At first you chalked it up to the natural conflicts all teens have as they make their way in life and in the world. But you knew it was more than that.

Your mind's rationalizations could no longer cover up the pain associated with the absence of your father. Your mind had tried to convince you that his absence was in fact a plus. It afforded you an opportunity to explore, you said to friends. It freed you to try new things without having that voice near, cautioning you to be careful, or telling you that it couldn't be done as fathers sometimes tend to do.

Until that point in your life, you had not recognized that his absence and your determination to do things on your own were, in fact, contributing to your separation from others, and from GOD. Do you not remember that little boy, all alone, determined to be the quarterback? I can still see him practicing by throwing a football through a bicycle tire hanging in a tree. That image still gives me a warm smile when I revisit it."

Phillip folded his hands softly in his lap and gently bowed his head. He let flow a long sigh. The image of that little boy produced a quiet sadness in him. He had not allowed himself to think of those times for quite a while. Tears welled in his eyes but he did not speak.

"The process continued in high school" said the old man. "As student body president, the riots that broke out during Black History month placed you squarely in the middle of the fracas. The inability to satisfy the frustrations of both the black and white communities pushed you further into isolation.

It was too much for teenager. I concede you that.

And yet you must concede that your mind loved the drama and conflict. It helped to justify the erroneous belief that you were alone. It helped your mind create a self who was separate from everyone else, and from GOD... a false self!

You were not alone, I assure you. You were developing habits that would one day complicate your life situation though. Your insistence on being in control and doing it alone has resulted in conflict all along the way. That separateness is what has put your life situation at odds with the natural rhythm of things."

"I didn't want it. I didn't want to be in control. I was just trying to survive. All I wanted was to finish high school and get on with my life."

"I understand that" offered the old man. Those kinds of circumstances are purported to "build character" and to make your path clearer. But I tell you this: 'the wind favors no ship that doesn't have a port'. You cannot operate outside the natural rhythm of things and expect to be successful. True success, true happiness is only achieved through cooperation. It is a collective effort.

It is no wonder that by the time you had reached college you had perfected your game face. You were completely separated from your feelings. Has not your mantra since then been that "it does not matter how I feel, it only matters that I do the right thing"? My question is: what is the right thing, and for whom? It clearly has not served you or any of the people you love. For if it did you would not be here today.

To approach life in that manner may appear selfless but it is the most selfish thing your mind can do. It robs your soul of the opportunity for love, truth, and joy. It separates you from other people, and from GOD.

The hint that things were drastically wrong should have occurred when your friend in the class a year ahead dropped out of school. He too had perfected his game face. And yet, even with that, the rest of you ignored the obvious and continued on like nothing had happened. It was never mentioned.

Not once. Even now, when you think of him you have refused to reach out. You speak of your desire to help others and yet you refuse to set aside your needs for theirs. Is not this the ultimate in selfishness? Is not this ultimate failure?"

Phillip did not answer. No answer was necessary. He accepted the old man's words for what they were. And what they were was truth.

"It was also during those years that your pain took on a monstrous persona. You incorporated the pain of an entire people, an entire culture into your psyche. You used the color of your skin to separate yourself from the rest of the population.

Your mind loved the drama. It loved the conflict. You loved the convenience of having a villain. It made it easier to isolate yourself. But I will tell you this: your mind would have arrived at the same conclusion regardless of your circumstances.

Your mind was in its glory. It had Information to analyze, problems to solve (and to create), and better yet, judgments to make.

That is what the mind does. It creates an identity, a false identity, based on past experiences and projects that identity into the future. In this way the mind is in control. You and I are no longer connected. You and GOD are no longer connected. You have been separated from your own soul and from BEING.

That is how you got here, and that is how you and others have forgotten your connection to each other and your connectedness to GOD. That is how all men have come to deny their connectedness to each other and to GOD.

Ironically, as you entered medical school and subsequently training in Plastic Surgery, you were completely isolated from everyone else. Your mind had succeeded in accomplishing that of which you were most afraid. You had become your game face.

Inside something was wrong and you could not escape the pain. Your soul was incomplete and there existed a feeling of abandonment that has always been your companion. You could not enjoy the moment's successes because your mind would only allow that they be seen as stepping stones into the future.

Your mind's obsession with some future salvation has never allowed you to connect on a spiritual level in the present. It has become a self-fulfilling prophecy: the more alone you become, the more your mind projects your happiness to somewhere or someone in the future, and hence, the more alone you become…and the more isolated.

Take your last real relationship. You view your break-up as desertion on the part of your girlfriend. But have you considered that your isolationism may have frustrated her efforts to be closer to you? Have you considered how difficult it must have been for her, wanting to be there for you, but being held at arm's length all along the way?"

"That's not true," Phillip stormed back pushing himself away from the table and standing to present a more imposing figure. The old man had finally accomplished a direct hit. Anger bubbled up from the depths of Phillip's soul. "I did everything I could possibly do for her. I made no demands that compromised who she was. All I was… was supportive."

"That you were. I grant you that. You have been more than honorable in a number of aspects of your life. I have no quarrel with who you are. I merely present those questions for perspective.

The issue at hand is not what you have done or failed to do. The issue at hand is your own happiness with your own life situation. I am merely suggesting that your problems may be the result of a single factor and that that factor is your lack of awareness of BEING, a lack of awareness of your connectedness to all other things."

"And to God?" Phillip interjected.

"Especially to GOD!" the old man shot back. "It's no wonder that by the time you entered private practice your isolation was complete. Think of it. You had few friends in your chosen field, no contact with the people who trained you (in spite of your love for them) and avoidance of anything extracurricular that would require contact with colleagues.

You are being used by your mind instead of you using it. Your mind loves the drama because it feeds a false sense of self. Furthermore, it separates you from who you are. It separates you from LOVE, TRUTH, and JOY. It separates you from BEING. That is the basis for not only your problems, but all of the world's problems.

You are not alone in your aloneness. Each of you may choose to view your circumstance as different. Each of you has taken your own path to arrive at the same destination. Nonetheless, the solution, the resolution of the pain which describes your life situation Is the same."

> WE ARE ONE, YOU AND I
> WE ARE NOT SEPARATE FROM EACH OTHER
> NOR ARE WE SEPERATE FROM GOD

Phillip finished the remainder of his dinner without speaking a word. The old man remained silent also, but never touched his food. He simply allowed the moment to be.

"Can you not see, "the old man offered after a long silence, "that that is how the fire started? Your separation from GOD and not any other calamity is what exposed your misery."

"I wish it were that simple" Phillip offered.

"It is that simple" the old man countered.

"Oh really... I was crucified in the press. It had nothing to do with GOD. Each day brought more venom than the day before. People were simply being mean, period."

"That's also true" the old man said. "People who are unconscious can be very mean indeed. Their separation from GOD, from BEING, does not allow them to see that what they do to another, they also do to themselves.

I am reminded of the words of your Henry David Thoreau. He wrote: "the finest qualities of our nature, like the bloom of fruits, can be preserved only by the most delicate of handling. Yet we do not treat ourselves, nor one another, thus tenderly".

"You've read Thoreau?"

"Of course, I have, and so have you. But pay particular attention to the part that suggests that sometimes we are not even gentle with ourselves. Most of what was taking place, was taking place in your mind. Your soul knew the truth."

"In my mind... you have to be joking... My soul knew the truth. What is that? ... The whole thing was a nightmare. It was horrible and I will not patronize you by saying it was the best thing that could have happened to me because it wasn't. It was the worst.

If my soul knew the TRUTH, it should have shared It with the rest of the world."

"It did..."

"It did what?"

"Your soul shared what it knew with the rest of the world. Yet do not blame your soul or yourself because the world was unreceptive. The world too is undergoing a process of enlightenment.

Phillip paused for a moment, "It's hard to let go. I feel violated. I'm constantly reminded of the horror of it all. It's just hard to let go. I guess that's sort of what got me here."

"No that is not what got you here. What got you here was the GRACE OF GOD. Left to your own devices you may never have arrived. The inability to let go is what keeps you here."

The old man was right and Phillip knew it. It was only through the GRACE of GOD that he was here. "That is wherever here is, exactly?"

The constant rehashing of the facts, at least Phillip's perceived notion of the facts, is what kept him sad and feeling wronged. There were times when it seemed that his brain would explode. Racing, negative thoughts haunted him during wakefulness and sleep.

His solution had been to quit, to end this life and be done with it. No one, who knew him, could have ever imagined that Phillip could have reached this point in his life. It was the antithesis of the projection of who he was. But the pressure, even for him, had become unbearable. He was forced to block out the noise. He could take it no longer.

Yet in the stillness he discovered his true self. He realized that he was not his mind, nor his body. Nor was he the collection of thoughts and experiences that had come to define him.

Initially, Phillip had experienced a sense of disorientation. When one first arrives on the other side of the fire, his world has changed. Things are no longer the way they were before. One's legs are wobbly like those of a child. He clings to the simplest of things in order to steady his way.

Phillip had come to search for patterns, for order everywhere in order to gain some control over his thoughts and his world: a sequence of numbers on a digital clock; the arrangement of books on a shelf; the color progression of shirts hanging in a closet; anything that would stop the chaos.

He also waited for the call that never came: that familiar voice that once gave purpose and hope to his life. A sadness developed that took him deeper within himself. Further and further he sank until ultimately, he reached a place of divine quiet.

In this place Phillip come to realize that he was never really alone. The call for which he had been wailing was not to come from without. It was to come from within. It was to be his SOUL claiming its rightful place in his existence.

Phillip's communication with BEING at that precise moment was nothing less than stupendous, miraculous, fantastic, amazing and yes… awe-inspiring. It was beautiful, empowering, serene, peaceful, blessed and joyful. Time, as he knew it, gave way to eternity. Knowledge was his in an instant. He could feel the connectedness of all things and came to cherish not only the objects but even the space within and between them. He came to recognize himself as that space. For that was his essence, the essence of GOD; the space that holds all things together.

Phillip remained there weightless and peaceful. He recognized this as experiencing the LOVE he had always known existed. The LOVE his SOUL had longed to feel once again. The LOVE he had forgotten.

His arrival on the other side of the fire had returned to him a PEACE and clarity that, he knew, in an instant, had to be shared. There was no other way to look at It. It did not belong to him alone.

The GRACE OF GOD had returned to his perspective.

At that same moment, he could recognize the voice of the old man once again speaking to him.

"I recognized that your first impulse, as it is for most people, was to engage in self-pity.

Your mind, demonstrating the scoundrel it is, was trying to re-establish itself as the dominant force in your life. The difference is this time you could see It coming. Take this opportunity to watch as your mind attempts to return to the patterns and tricks it has used in the past to gain control. Study him. He will return time and time again. Throughout the remainder of your life, your mind will attempt to wrestle control from your soul. You will notice it as an impulse not sponsored by LOVE. Be ever vigilant for that is the battle going on inside you."

Phillip acknowledged the old man's wisdom but only smiled. Once you have walked through the fire and come out on the other side you have been changed. The focus required to endure momentarily turns off your mind. It is then that you get a glimpse of the feeling of BEING. In the stillness, you are touched by LOVE, TRUTH, JOY, and PEACE.

Things become much clearer. There is no turning back. You come to feel, to understand, that all things are connected.

Life cannot go back to the way it was before.

The choice is not simply what to do next? It is much bigger and brighter than that. It is how to be?

How do you relate to your new understanding? What is there to do when you finally remember that you are a divine part of a divine whole?

The artificial separation of you and me no longer exists. We are no longer separate from each other nor are we separate from GOD.

> **YOU DON'T HAVE TO DO,
> JUST BE!**

As Phillip considered the questions raised by his new understanding, his eyes began to water. He was content. No longer was he caught up in his own distracting thoughts. His path was becoming clearer. He could see that his true salvation lies in the spiritual truths of which the old man spoke.

The old man gently placed his hand on Phillip's shoulder. "It is good that you are in touch with your feelings he said. "For feeling is the language of the SOUL. Feeing is the language of GOD. Go within. Realize that the answers to all your questions are inside of you.

Close your eyes. Clear your mind. Feel yourself breath. Notice the rhythmic movement of your abdomen. Feel your heart beating. Experience the blood flowing through your arteries. Feel the tingling in your toes as each cell announces that it is alive. Enter that void inside of you where there is stillness. Embrace the peace associated with your connectedness to all things. Experience the reality that you are a part of BEING."

Phillip did as the old man instructed. He stopped resisting. He made the conscious effort to accept the universal flow and rhythm of life. He allowed himself to relinquish his position. He opened his heart to other truths. The sacrifice of his own selfish perspective was the way to his happiness. Surrender was the path to constructive change.

"Most people who are not conscious," the old man began, "believe that arrival at BEING is a time for action. It is not. Your improved level of consciousness is best served by silence. You don't have to do, just be. It is best to allow your SOUL space and time to become the dominant voice within you. You must develop the ability to watch and monitor your own thoughts. All that you think and therefore all that you do must be motivated in LOVE.

"How am I to do that?" Phillip asked.

"Simply shut off your mind. Anticipate your next thought but never allow it to arrive. Things will become easier as your thoughts and actions are in harmony with life's greater purpose, rather than opposed to it. You are able to count your blessings, not your problems. You develop your strengths and give your dreams the chance to come true. You come to realize that there is indeed a huge difference between doing and being."

Phillip resolved to suspend his own thoughts and to listen to the words of the old man. Only this time he was committed to feeling the words not just hearing them. They required no pasteurization on his part. They were to be taken for what they were. And although he had heard the words many times before, listening to the old man now allowed the words to take on their full meaning.

"Doing is what your body is engaged in," the old man said. "Being can only be described as a function of the soul. The soul, indeed life itself, is eternal. The soul exists regardless of what the body is doing. Life is eternal, death is the illusion."

"Wow, that's an interesting take on it!"

"It is indeed. But I would venture to say that all TRUTH Is interesting. If you want to discover the TRUTH, look at how you feel about a thing. Feelings can be hard to identify and even harder to accept. But hidden in your feelings are your most profound TRUTHS. The natural rhythm of things and the path to self-realization is riddled with wonderment. One need only grasp the magnificence of being."

"That I do get." Phillip offered. "Clearly a hundred years from now it won't matter what I was doing today or did for a living… at least not to my soul. Ultimately, my soul, which incidentally will be the only thing to survive, will only care about what I was being while I was doing what I was doing."

"Exactly!"

" I guess that is what is meant by it is what it is."

'Right again" the old man said. "The secret, however, is in having passion for the process. The joy is in approaching each moment with the anticipation of a child. What splendor will today bring? What discovery will I have in this moment that demonstrates the utter magnificence of life? Sometimes in order to find yourself, it is important to go back to where you lost your way. For you Phillip that is back to your childhood. For mankind, it is a bit further.

If you will take this spiritual journey with me, I am sure your path will become evident."

"I don't really have a choice, do I?" Phillip asked.

"There is always a choice." the old man countered. "You need only accept the choice that serves you. And what serves you will ultimately be to base your actions on SPIRITUAL TRUTHS, not human experience. That is of course if you choose to be happy."

"I certainly want happiness, but to be honest, I'd settle for feeling fulfilled."

"I'm glad you said that" the old man countered. "Fulfillment is indeed the place to start. It is the foundation of happiness.

"Think first in terms of creation. In your beginning, that is the beginning of man, GOD, that which IS {as mystics say), Is all there was and there was nothing else. I am of course speaking cosmically."

"There was only the energy, the spirit, which man calls GOD."

"I get it," said Phillip.

"Yet GOD could not truly know himself because all that IS, is all that was, and there was nothing else.

And so, all that IS, was not. For in the absence of something else, all that IS, is not."

"That was quite a mouthful," Phillip joked.

"It is that and more. Now GOD was aware that HE was all there was, but this was not enough. He wanted more. He needed more. He needed not only to know that HE was wonderful. He needed to feel it. And so, GOD produced from himself all that exists. HIS purpose for you, and for life, is that you should know yourself as GOD. That you come to know yourself and all that exists as a part of him and that you come to recognize your own magnificence."

"Well, none of us Is doing a good job at that" offered Phillip. "Just look around. There is war and hatred everywhere."

"There is also LOVE and caring but I do get your point. Men must come to realize that they are one: That all men, as GOD, said before "ARE A DIVINE PART of A DIVINE WHOLE". It is the soul's desire to turn its grandest concept about itself into its greatest experience. That is your purpose. It is your soul's purpose."

"Then why aren't we getting on with It?" "Who says you are not?"

"I say we are not. Have you taken a nice hard look at the state, the world is in?"

"Have you taken a nice soft one? The turmoil that you see is merely a result of the shift in consciousness on the part of man. It is a shift that must occur if man is to evolve. The only requirement is FAITH...If you have but the faith of a mustard seed, you shall move mountains"

"I've heard that one before.

"You've heard it but have you lived it? GOD has said IT, and countless preachers have repeated it, that "IT"...whatever you choose IT to be... "Is there because GOD has said it is there. Even before you ask, GOD shall have answered: that whatsoever you shall choose, choosing it in the name of GOD, so shall it be. That is THE PROMISE OF GOD."

"I choose for this nightmare to end."

"That is a wise decision. I was wondering when you would get there."

"I have always been there."

"No, actually you haven't. And if you truly believe you have, then you have missed the beauty, the utter magnificence, of our interaction. Simply choosing does not mean that you will have all you ask for. Nor can you have anything you want. The very nature of asking suggests that it is not so. GOD created laws that govern man's world. Thoughts, words, and actions are productive. Simply asking does not make it so.

For a thing to really be manifest, you must also know that it is so. When you thank GOD in advance for that which you choose to experience, you in effect acknowledge that it is there. Thankfulness is, therefore, the most powerful statement to GOD."

"Okay, thank GOD this nightmare is over."

"That is a good start, but your cynicism knows no boundary. Gratitude cannot be used as a tool with which to manipulate GOD. You cannot lie to yourself. Your soul knows the truth of your thoughts.

GOD created you in the image and likeness of GOD. You have created the rest. GOD has given you free choice to do with life as you will.

You need only determine what your soul will be being while your mind and body are doing. That is the first step in changing tragedy into triumph."

> ACCEPT THE PROMISE OF GOD

"Don't ignore that thoughts and words are creative" the old man said to Phillip. "If you want something to happen that is what you get: wanting. If you wish a thing to be a certain way, that is what you get: wishing. For GOD has said millions of times in a million different ways: not that you shall have everlasting life, but that you do; not that you shall have whatever it is that you ask for, but that you do; and not that you and GOD shall be one, but that you are."

Phillip had heard these words many, many times before. However, he could not shake the feeling that something was missing.

"There is nothing missing" the old man offered.

"Why do you keep doing that?"

"I keep doing It because you keep doing it "

"While words are one way in which GOD speaks to us, HE also uses thoughts, feelings, pictures, and premonitions. Whatever it takes is what GOD uses. You said earlier it is not to whom GOD speaks, but who listens."

"What now? Are you going to use my own words against me?"

"They are your words. My point is simply that there is nothing missing. You have all you need to accomplish whatever it is that you choose to accomplish. For GOD has made it that way. You cannot fail."

"Funny, I feel like I've failed already. Surely this is not success."

"It could be," the old man shot back. "It really depends on how you choose to look at it. Which, by the way, brings me back to my original point: There is nothing missing. That has been the difficult part for you to accept. Your failure to accept the PROMISE OF GOD is the problem. It is why you feel unconnected, alone, unsuccessful, and a failure.

As a child you learned to find acceptable in yourself that which your parents, particularly your mother, found acceptable. As a school kid you found acceptable in yourself that which your teachers found acceptable. As a teenager you found acceptable in yourself what other teens found acceptable in you. As an adult you have come to find acceptable in yourself that which society says is acceptable.

Your search for self-worth has been, at best backwards."

"What do you mean backwards?"

"Your search for peace and salvation has been from outside sources. The answer has always been within you. You have sought your salvation in what you do, or whom you're with.

GOD has created you, just as he has created this world, to be complete. Everything you seek from outside sources: love, truth, companionship is already present in you. There is everything need to support all life on this planet. There is enough. You need only remember the PROMISE OF GOD!"

"You keep saying that. What," Phillip demanded, "is the PROMISE OF GOD?"

The old man smiled, "That's an easy one. You need only to quiet the noise that is the needless activity of your mind. You need only to listen to your soul."

"Again?" Phillip asked. "How often am I supposed to do that?"

"As often as you can," the old man answered; "as many times a day as you choose. Always!

Life is a process of creation as GOD has said before. But you cannot be creative unless, or rather until, you turn off your mind and listen to your soul. Every great artist knows this."

"That may be true but I am a scientist. I need facts and data."

"There is a place for facts and data. But they are about observation, not creation. Creation requires that your soul taps into the rhythm of life. Creation requires that you allow discovery to come from within."

"Okay. Okay, I get it."

With that Phillip began to concentrate on his breathing.

"Wait," the old man interrupted. "You have done that before. That is one way, but it is not the only way to quiet your mind.

There are many ways to achieve this focus, this connection BEING. Athletes achieve it when they are "in the zone". Business executives achieve it when they are so involved in a report that hours pass like seconds. You have experienced it many times yourself. Have you not been so involved in work that everything else in the room seemed to melt away leaving only you and the object of your focus?"

Phillip had experienced that state many times before. Even now as he concentrated on the old man's words, his entire perspective changed. He hung there, somewhere between the physical and the spiritual worlds, and yet with the ability to experience both.

In the stillness was the PEACE he had experienced before. His companions in this place included LOVE, TRUTH and JOY. They existed without their opposites. He knew then that he had entered the world of the absolute, the world of his soul, the world of GOD.

Phillip was acutely aware of his surroundings and yet they did not impose themselves on him. The old man's laboratory seemed more vivid than it had just moments before. The sunlight coming through the window carried more than just light, it carried warmth and life.

He concentrated not so much on the chairs, or desk, or walls, but rather on the space between them. That which held the room together was now his focus. Everything seemed to be just a bit more alive.

"The PROMISE OF GOD", the old man began, "Is that we, you and I and GOD, will not be separated forever. The PROMISE OF GOD is that we are one, there is enough and you don't have to do, just BE.

The PROMISE OF GOD is that YOU can achieve all that you can conceive. There is only one purpose for all of life, and that is for you and all that lives to experience the fullest glory of BEING. Life is an opportunity for one to know practically what one already knows conceptually: that they and GOD are one. That is the PROMISE OF GOD.

Acceptance of THE PROMISE OF GOD IS the second step in changing tragedy into triumph."

> **SELF AWARENESS IS THE GOAL**

Phillip shook his head in self-disgust, "I have been incredibly stupid, haven't I?"

"Stupid is unfair," said the old man. "Perhaps it would be better to say that you have been so busy at trying to live the "right" way that you have failed, up to this point, to really live at all.

In your attempt to create a perfect world for those you love, you have missed life's simple purpose. What satisfaction can be found in a life devoted to giving your children everything, if while pursuing those things, you miss the process of your children growing to be young adults?

You have ignored the simple pleasures that would have given your life so much more meaning and joy. You have missed that joy lies not in the result, but in the process itself."

"I really haven't missed it, believe me. I just felt that I needed to bring more to the table than high hopes."

"Oh, really? Have you not prepared your entire life to take to your hometown the jobs it needs to survive? Has not that been your wish?

Yet would it have not been better to be there working alongside the people of that town all along. That is where satisfaction is to be found. How can you know what they need, if you do not listen to them? How can you help them, if you do not know their goals?"

The old man began to soften and a smile cam over his face. "Take refuge in the knowledge that your journey is not through. There will always be the opportunity for you to choose the path that leads to peace and salvation. For that is also the PROMISE OF GOD. It is never too late.

The important idea to grasp here is that the goal is awareness. That is the all-important third step in changing tragedy into triumph."

The old man turned directly to Phillip. "Phillip," he began. "Let me tell you something that will be of importance to you from this day forward. The way you felt yesterday is not the way it always has to be. Things can change and you have the power to change them. You need but connect with BEING and in the stillness the answers will come.

GOD has created a wonderful world where each of us has the ability to create any experience we choose."

"Choose" interrupted Phillip. "How can that be? I'm not sure that I am ready to swallow that I chose this."

"Perhaps not literally, no, but surely you can see how your own choices and decisions have lead you here. Think of it this way: GOD, in creating our world, also established laws that define how things work. Whether you are conscious of it or not, you have been operating within these laws all of your life. Everything that you have created thus far is the result of them.

Man consists of three parts: soul, mind, and body. Each has a purpose and each exists as part of the whole. The three aspects of man viewed creatively can also be called thought, word, and action.

The process of creation starts with a thought. Everything that exists in our world began as someone's thought. The phone, the computer, and the automobile at one time existed only in someone's imagination.

The second level of creation occurs when those thoughts are brought to life through words. The simple act of writing it down, of drawing up plans, elevates a thought to a higher creative level.

The final step in creation is action. Action makes manifest in the physical world the fruits of our thoughts.

Consistently monitor your thoughts for they are creative. Be certain they are in harmony with who you choose to be. Your mind will attempt to play tricks on you in order to gain control:

THINK ABOUT WHAT YOU THINK ABOUT!

That is enlightenment!

Your thoughts are destined to one day produce your reality. Do not take them lightly. Monitor them. Can you honestly say that your predicament is not the result of your mind's habitual thoughts? Can you truly say that your predicament was not the result of your unhappiness, but rather the other way around? Did not your unhappiness cause you to abandon your enthusiasm for your work? Did not your lack of enthusiasm cause you to fantasize about other careers? Does not thinking about quitting mean that you already have?"

Phillip stood there stunned. The old man's words had iron. They cut through his false sense of self like a chain saw through butter. He had been laid open and the only thing before him was the TRUTH.

"You must ask yourself," the old man continued, "If you are willing to move forward by sacrificing your own expectations. You must ask yourself if you are willing to voluntarily surrender to the PROMISE OF GOD in order to gain enlightenment, and a greater sense of awareness. Can you set aside your own needs for the needs of others? Can you honestly and completely come to know and accept that things are the way they are because you have chosen them to be that way?

The process begins with your commitment to this idea. You cannot fool yourself. You cannot lie to yourself. True control begins with awareness. There is none as blind as he who just refuses to see.

Take inventory of your surroundings. Monitor your thoughts and your feelings to be certain they represent you and who you want to be. Let not any emotion you have be as much a surprise to you as to the object of your emotion. Seek not to control your feelings, embrace them.

> **ACCEPT AND OWN ALL THAT YOU CREATE**

It did not take a genius to see where the old man was headed here. The fourth leg of Phillip's journey in changing tragedy into triumph was an idea he had wrestled with before. Intellectually, he understood that things were the way they were for him because he had chosen them to be that way. Personal responsibility had always been a recurring theme with him. However he could not shake the feeling that somehow this was beyond his view of personal responsibility. He had always been able to convince himself that that was exactly what he had been doing, taking responsibility. But being confronted at this moment by the old man was undeniable proof that he hadn't.

He hadn't taken responsibility for his actions. He had merely washed his hands of blame.

True responsibility contained a few more layers. The essence lay a bit deeper and his inability to accurately define responsibility was complicated by his own irrational, negative thoughts about himself.

Certainly, he had his faults as all human beings do. And surely, he had known disaster. But Phillip also knew that while he could be completely objective, indeed, kind and generous in assessing other people's faults, he was vindictive and cruel in assessing his own.

"That is also why you are here Phillip" the old man offered. "Your own self-hatred, a system of self- reinforcing negative thoughts and feelings, is what took you to that window. Your involvement is related IN TIME to an unfortunate event, but your involvement was not the CAUSE of that event. Three months of investigation by the authorities should surely have confirmed that for you."

"I know," admitted Phillip. "Intellectually, I get it. But there is a part of me that won't let go. Don't get me wrong…"

"Don't worry, I can't get you wrong," interrupted the old man.

Phillip shook his head in mock disgust but continued anyway. "I realize that people die every day. And, although this may seem a bit harsh on the surface... frankly, I don't care. That doesn't mean that I don't...That's why I... feel so miserable now even knowing that it wasn't me at fault..."

The old man stared in disbelief. "What was that?" he joked. "A little tongue-tied are we?"

"What I'm trying to say, and not very well, is that I care deeply about people. I chose the profession I did for precisely that reason. It's really how I have come to define myself: by what I do for others. But more importantly I care that I do the right thing for each patient. Life and death is a thing for GOD. My job is to do the right thing."

"And you did!"

"Yeah, but I couldn't help but be aghast at people's reactions."

"Well, actually you could help it. You control the focus of your mind, but I get your point."

"I couldn't believe people, the press in particular. Do people really think that the doctor isn't invested in his patients? I'm so disgusted with people I could spit. For Christ's sake..."

"Good Choice!"

Phillip ignored that. "For Christ's sake, most patients become my friends. I have just as much, maybe more, interest in the outcome than they do.

Patients tell me things and share information about how they feel, and what they want, that they wouldn't discuss with their husband, or best friend."

"That is indeed true."

"But here's me catch, at least as far as I'm concerned: the secret to being a great doctor is the ability to listen. That's responsibility. People may not know what you call it, or what the treatment is, but if you listen to them, they will tell you what's wrong. The doctor simply has to listen and believe in what they are saying."

"That is true also, but what exactly is your point?

"This nightmare has changed all of that for me. Former patients came out of the woodwork to tell lies. I don't think I could ever sit across from a patient again and feel comfortable believing that I could trust them and worse yet…what they are saying."

"You don't have to… TRUST IN GOD instead."

"What does that mean?"

"It means exactly what I said. This may be difficult for you to accept, but you have put too much faith in other people's words. Words are the worst way to communicate because they are only approximations for feelings. They are not the feeling, only descriptions of it."

"That's not very comforting you know. I accepted my connectedness to all things. Now it sounds like you are saying but don't trust people or what they have to say."

"I'm not saying that at all. I'm merely pointing out some of the limitations of the physical world in relation to BEING. People in the physical world are also in the process of remembering who they are. Many, indeed most, have failed to evolve as of yet. They are not living a conscious life. One cannot expect a conscious under those circumstances. The same pertains to responsibility.

Understanding the scope of responsibility requires much more than thinking. It requires feeling, and acceptance of increasing duty. As one elevates his consciousness, so too must he elevate his level of responsibility."

If Phillip was to acquire the tools necessary for turning tragedy into triumph, he would need a clear understanding of this essential step. No longer would it be appropriate for Phillip to review an issue only in terms of its effect on him. Responsibility requires that you also consider the impact on all things: another individual, a tree, the soil, a river, a lake, the ocean, the continent, the earth, the atmosphere and the cosmos: all of it. That is true responsibility.

Phillip had become consumed with looking at the ten percent of his life that was less than perfect, and ignoring the ninety percent that was. This way of thinking, of looking at the world, was no longer acceptable with his new level of awareness demanded it.

"Why did all this have to happen? I don't deserve his" he said to the old man.

What makes you say that?" The old man asked. "Perhaps you do deserve this. Perhaps you do deserve this opportunity to be closer to GOD. It's really about how you choose to see it don't you think?

Responsibility isn't just accountability. It's also about determining if the outcome speaks to who you are and who you want to be. It's about choosing to make a thing better when you are not culpable. Responsibility also speaks to the connectedness of all things. It speaks to BEING."

"Yeah, I get what you are saying. I get it. I just don't get why it's happening to me."

"That's an easy one. It's happening to you because you believe you are not good enough to be a part of GOD."

"But I'm not GOD."

"I didn't say that you believe that you aren't good enough to be God. I said to be a part of God."

Your separation from BEING was so complete that you had forgotten who you are. Yet this is no Accident. It is all part of a Divine plan. Who better to demonstrate the emptiness of life without a Connectedness to GOD than someone who appears to have it all?

"Now you've got to be joking. I certainly didn't have it all."

"Actually, you do. You've just forgotten that.

You also have the desire to make the world better. You have the desire to demonstrate that we are all one. Here's another secret. You cannot create who you want to be if you are already him. It is, and was, necessary that you see yourself as separate from GOD in order to experience your connection to GOD by creating it completely.

And GOD is in cahoots with you. It is a partnership. For GOD wants for you what you want for you."

'Yeah and…"

"And now you have that opportunity.

There have been many times when you have realized that the problems for mankind lie not in what they do, but in their failure to be. Have you not said many times that the solution to the world's problems are for man to realize that we are all one; that there is enough; and that the greatest disease that is the scourge of man is not cancer or heart disease, but hate? Have you not said these things?"

"Yes, I have."

"Well then, has not all that has happened given you the opportunity to create who you are and who you want to be in this instance? Is this not the gift from GOD that you seek?

You are focused on what you see as the negative. But it would be infinitely more useful for you to focus on the opportunity at hand.

That is responsibility. The real question is not "why is this happening to me", but how can I use what is happening to me to create the most glorious version of who I know myself to be. Focus on creating the circumstances of your life that you would like to experience. That is the key.

"Our meeting then was really just a part of GOD'S PLAN."

"It all is."

"I need to do some SOUL searching."

"Yes you do and yes you did. You also needed to come to this moment as a child, an individual with no preconceived notion of what is, or what is not. You needed once again to see the possibilities. If you can remember to do that you will understand the full scope of responsibility.

You will be able to create all the things you want, rather than recreate the problems of the past."

"I see it now" offered Phillip. "I see clearly how I got here. I create the circumstances of my life; not some of them but all of them. I must take responsibility for all of them so that I might change some of them.

The only tool required is to think about the things I think about. For my thoughts are creative. I need only believe in the PROMISE OF GOD. I don't have to do, I just have to be."

> **CHERISH THE MAGNIFICENCE OF THE PRESENT MOMENT**

"Yes" said the old man, "I believe you have it. There is but one more idea to grasp."

Phillip smiled with anticipation. Along with awareness came an energy that had transformed him. He was not the man he had been before. He was his more positive self. There was an air of confidence that surrounded him. He seemed taller though that was impossible. His breaths were deeper and his face fuller. He had truly been transformed.

"The next great obstacle on your path to triumph is to conquer the illusion of time."

"Time," Phillip asked "why time?"

"Just as GOD created man as a three-part being, so to have men created time as three parts: there is the past, the future, and the present.

For you, and indeed for most human beings, to be in the present moment is a very difficult thing. You define yourselves through your past, and you project your happiness into your future. Your minds and bodies are the culprits.

You ignore that all things take place in the present moment. There was no past, and there will be no future. There is only that which takes place right now.

This instant was sent to you as a gift from GOD. In this moment is the TRUTH for which your soul yearns. Accept this moment for what it is. If you begin to analyze it, to dissect it, you will find that in an instant, it is gone."

"Are you saying that time is somehow bad? That doesn't make sense."

"I'm not saying that time is bad. Oh, quite to the contrary. I am saying the notion of time is very useful. But always remain cognizant of the fact that time is a mental construct, an illusion if you will. Time is a tool which man created to manage the physical world.

The problem arises when the illusion becomes your reality, that is when the illusion becomes synonymous with your mind and with the process of thinking."

"And that is a problem because…"

"Because allowing an illusion to be your reality allows your mind to once again be in control. Your soul is your essence. It is your connection to BEING. The soul must be the director of your thoughts and actions, not your mind.

The soul knows that you and GOD are one. The mind will deny that. The soul understands and acknowledges this instant. It recognizes that it is sent from GOD. Your mind, because it cannot grasp this TRUTH, will not allow this moment to be.

Have you not witnessed a life defined by an accomplishment, or a tragedy, in the past: the high school athlete, the prom queen, or the actress whose only part was in the high school play?

The past is their identity and because of it, they cannot grasp the magnificence of this moment.

Or likewise there is the intellectual who for fifteen years has been planning to write the definitive novel. Or the housewife who will one day return to medical school to obtain that degree that she delayed in order to take care of her children. They both seek their salvation in the future.

Worse is the man who married the love of his life at twenty. He then worked two jobs for forty years in preparation for the wonderful life they would enjoy together in their twilight years. Only the problem is the object of his love passed away the day he retired."

"I see," said Phillip. "They all are missing the most wonderful, and magnificent…and yes, sacred thing of all: right now."

"Precisely! IF ONE IS TO CHANGE TRAGEDY INTO TRIUMPH, ONE MUST LIVE IN THE PRESENT MOMENT."

"I have heard that said many times before and in many different ways," Phillip offered. "People have said the only place is here and the only time is now".

Buddhists have quite astutely offered: "if not now, then when".

Every philosophy and every school of thought have offered some adage about being in the present moment. I guess I really never got it until now."

"Now is fine. Better late than never, I always say."

"Man, you are something."

"And so are you! Nonetheless, it is very important that we are clear. In reality, this moment is all there is. There is nothing else. The future and the past are illusions. The present moment is sacred. Through the present moment you can transcend the confines of the mind and body and enter the absolute world of the soul, that place of BEING where you are one with GOD. You could not do it in the past and you will not do it in the future. It can only happen in this moment."

"I get it" said Phillip. "We are all a divine part of a divine whole. We are one you and I. We are not separate from each other, nor are we separate from GOD.

GOD speaks to all of us, all the time. SHE comes to us in an instant, providing in as many ways as we can imagine, all the things we need. Simply accept the PROMISE OF GOD.

Own all that you create. For that is responsibility.

There is enough to support life on this planet and happiness within your SOUL. There is nothing to do, just be.

If we choose to recognize these facts, and are willing to give ourselves over to them, our lives will be fuller in every regard. One need only have the courage to believe it, and the daring to expect it."

"You have listened well," said the old man. "My work here is done, but yours is just beginning. You must continue on your journey, for as I said before, you are only half-way home. From this day forth share your passion, and help a soul that has lost its way."

Epilogue

As I listened to Phillip's story I was haunted by one very important detail. I couldn't figure out who was telling the story. At first I thought it was the old man but his reference to himself as "the old man" made absolutely no sense. Who speaks of themselves in the third person?

I convinced myself that it must be Phillip, but that made no sense either. Phillip appeared to be as much on a journey of remembrance and enlightenment as me. Every question, every detail of his growth, of his grasp of the concept of BEING, was happening to me at exactly the instant it was happening to him. Phillip clearly was not sharing his knowledge of a thing, but was allowing me to experience it with him. I am grateful for his kindness.

Phillip's story reminded me of the times when I have felt alone, sad, or helpless. Particularly poignant was his declaration that he felt he could no longer live with himself.

Phillip's mind had created an entity, a self, which was incongruent with his soul. His soul refused to live, confined to his body, with that entity present. His soul recognized that entity as unkempt and wanted no part of it.

I have felt that way at times. I suspect we all have. I Am grateful to Phillip for exposing that scoundrel in me. I am now better equipped to deal with my own demons. I am now better prepared to recognize my false self, and to limit his influence before he engages in activities in which my true self wants no part.

Phillip's soul is the author of his story. I should say THE SOUL is the author because the notion of Phillip's soul or mine makes no sense in light of what I have come to know: There is only ONE soul and we are all a part.

That explains the clearness of his words and his message. It also explains why I and everyone else who chooses to read Phillip's story, experiences BEING at the same time Phillip experiences it. The language of the soul is FEELING and TRUTH, and its Meaning is instantaneous.

While the mind and body have their place in remembering who we are, the essence of BEING lies with our SOUL. That is where the answers lie.

We are one, you and I. we are not separate from each other, nor are we separate from GOD. There is enough. You don't have to do, JUST BE.

"Therefore, be a light unto the darkness, and curse it not. Forget not who you are in the moment of your encirclement by that which you are not. Inquire within, rather than without. For the experience you create is the statement of who you are and who you choose to be. Know that what you do in the time of your greatest trial, can be the creation of your greatest triumph."

YHWH

A Spiritual Guide
Turning Tragedy into Triumph

Jan R. Adams M.D plastic surgeon, author, TV personality, lecturer, motivation speaker, and entrepreneur, attended Harvard University and the Ohio State University College of Medicine. His post-graduate medical training included the general surgery residency at the Lenox Hill Hospital, in New York City, where he served as the Chief surgical resident. He completed his residency in Plastic Surgery at the University of Michigan and a one- year fellowship in Aesthetic Surgery at UCLA School of Medicine. He then served as a Clinical Instructor in Plastic and Reconstructive Surgery at UCLA Hospitals.

Dr. Jan began his TV career as an on-air correspondent on EXTRA, the entertainment magazine show, and later co-hosted NBC's THE OTHER HALF, a male version of THE VIEW, along with Dick Clark, Danny Bonaduce, and Mario Lopez. Dr. Jan also hosted COSMETIC SURGERY LIVE A television event" in the United Kingdom and, for five years, was the face and authority of Discovery Health Channel's PLASTIC SURGERY: BEFORE AND AFTER, consistently one of the highest rated series on the network. He has appeared on numerous TV shows including OPRAH, SALLY, and as an expert contribution for ABC, MSNBC, and CNN.

In 2000 he published his first book, "EVERYTHING WOMEN OF COLOR SHOULD KNOW ABOUT COSMETIC SURGERY.

This was followed in 2005 by the launch of his TOTAL SKIN CARE SYSTEM FOR WOMEN OF COLOR in all 5400 Walgreens stores.

At the present time he is completing his next book:" Sometimes the Dragon Wins". He lives in Southern California.

www.ingramcontent.com/pod-product-compliance
Lightning Source LLC
LaVergne TN
LVHW021735060526
838200LV00052B/3293